Based on Science and Experience

By Brent A. Anders, Ph.D.

Professor / Life-Long Learner / Life-Long Student

How to Be a Super Student:
Based on Science and Experience

By Brent A. Anders, Ph.D.
University Professor,
U.S. Army Instructor, Sergeant Major *(Retired)*
Life-Long Learner / Life-Long Student

Editing Assistance By
Eva M. Anders

© Copyright 2021 by Brent A. Anders, Ph.D., Sovorel Publishing. All Rights Reserved.

Published by Sovorel Publishing Co., www.sovorelpublishing.com. This book is protected by international copyright law. No portion of this book may be reproduced without permission from the publisher, except as permitted by U.S. copyright law. For special permissions contact: Contact@SovorelPublishing.com.

Note that any websites described in this book may have disappeared or changed since this book was published. While the author and publisher have diligently prepared this book, neither of them makes any warranties or representations as to the accuracy or completeness of the contents of this manuscript after publication due to issues beyond their control. The strategies and advice contained within this book may not be suitable for all situations. Neither the author nor the publisher shall be liable for any loss of profit, health, or any other type of damages.

ISBN: 978-0-9987637-4-3 (digital), 978-0-9987637-5-0 (regular)

Keywords/Tags: learning, student, effective learning, study skills, student excellence, communication, motivation, participation, reflection, education, superpowers, academic success, studying, test taking

Dedicated to my beautiful family, Nelli, Eva, & Lileth, my Lord and savior Jesus Christ, hardworking librarians, and students everywhere.

To help my students and students around the world. I believe in you and together I know that you can all succeed. – And remember, learning is for life!

How to Be a Super Student:
Based on Science and Experience

Table of Contents

Introduction

Welcome hero. You are about to unlock the secrets of how **YOU** can gain the power to become a Super Student. By Super Student I specifically mean someone that can truly learn the material, get high grades (score well), and do so in an efficient way to have time for other important events and activities. This book was purposely written to be short and as easy to read as possible so that you can effortlessly and quickly learn the key concepts to becoming a Super Student.

Everyone reading this book can enhance their capabilities (academic superpowers) simply by implementing one of these key concepts but note that there is a synergistic and multiplicative effect when all concepts are implemented. The superpowers gained will help you succeed regardless of whether you are a face-to-face or online student.

The formula of this book: each key concept (superpower) will be presented, described, the importance will be given, and then it will be fully explained, showing how it can be practically incorporated into your learning process.

This book incorporates lessons learned from my own experience as a student, a soldier, a certified military instructor, and a university professor. My personal educational path has allowed me to gain many insights into learning while achieving a bachelor's degree in psychology, a master's degree in instructional technology, a Ph.D. in the field of education, as well as attending 1000's of face-to-face and online classes in the U.S. Army and graduating from the prestigious U.S. Sergeants' Major Academy. I also spent 15 years as a certified military instructor facilitating various courses for U.S. Soldiers and internationally for U.S. allies.

I have spent over 20 years in the field of higher education, working as an educational media consultant and as a university professor teaching both online and face-to-face courses. Due to this wide breadth and depth of education and experience, I have seen many different education styles and processes which have helped me in identifying the best insights/advice for this book. Finally, this book cites many different psychology and learning science research articles and books, as well as real student feedback that adds even more validity to the information presented.

I truly believe that following the guidance in this book will make you an excellent Super Student!

Superpower #1: BE YOUR FUTURE BEST FRIEND - *Time-Manipulation*

Description: Do things now to help your future self. Do things like study and work on the assignment now, in the present, to make it easier and better for your future self (be your own best friend in this way).

Importance: It is important to understand this idea/capability in that it will help to motivate you to accomplish all the other concepts (achieve the other superpowers) within this book. By thinking about and helping the near-future version of yourself you will gain so much more time and reduce so much stress that occurs when waiting until the last second to do something.

Explanation: The idea with this superpower concept is to think about your near future self. Notice how I said, "near future self." I'm not talking about the person you will be after graduation, after you get your first big job, or after you get married. I'm talking about you a few weeks from now; think about that person and be a best friend to that version of yourself. Do you want that person to be failing, falling behind, or stressing out because they haven't done an assignment or studied for that test tomorrow? Only you can help that future version of yourself by doing work now. – *Perceiving myself and time in this way has greatly assisted me in achieving academic success and will also empower you.*

Obtaining this superpower will help you avoid making statements such as

> *"I wish I could go back in time and start this assignment earlier, It's 2 AM and I'm still studying for my test tomorrow."*
>
> *"I should have started studying way before today,"* or even *"I wish I had done my assignment earlier so I could go to that party tonight."*

By thinking about your future self now, you will save yourself so much grief later on.

You need to perceive this as a sort of *time-manipulation superpower*. By taking the small amount of time now to follow all the concepts presented in this book you will greatly help that near-future version of yourself. Let the following be some powerful self-actualizing questions for you:

> *"Is what I am going to do now going to help my future self or hurt my future self?"*
>
> *"Am I being a good best friend to myself or not?"*

Keep these questions in mind as we go through the following concepts to help keep you and your near-future self on track and self-motivated to succeed and become the Super Student you are meant to be!

Remember that you, and you alone, are the only one who can fully take control of your learning. By releasing these superpowers within you, you will gain even greater control and ability to succeed.

Superpower #2: BE ORGANIZED

– Super Speed Powers

Description: This is the process of putting things (events/tasks/items) in a planned (organized) structure so that they can be easily and quickly obtained, observed, understood, remembered, and accomplished.

Importance: By knowing where things are (your learning materials and your assignments) it will make your life much easier and reduce your stress levels. In the same way, by organizing/scheduling your time, you will avoid costly surprises, be much more efficient, and have time available for other important things besides schoolwork.

Explanation: Being organized comes up again and again in learning science research as the number one way to succeed academically (Adams, & Blair, 2019; Hoops, & Artrip, 2016; Young, et al., 2019; Yu, et al., 2020). There are two aspects to this superpower of being organized: properly putting things in their place (*Organizing Items*) so that you can have them and use them when needed, and scheduling everything (*Organizing Time*) to achieve proper time management.

Organizing Items: Properly organize your content into folders and subfolders with proper titles so that it can be easily and quickly identified and/or searched for. Take photos of written notes as a backup. Store copies of your assignments on a backup drive as well as in the cloud. One technique I use is to email myself an assignment (different drafts and the final version) to ensure that I do not lose or misplace the information (especially if something were to happen to my laptop).

*__Great tools for this are:__ Google Drive, Microsoft OneDrive, DropBox, and Mega

*__Organize your digital devices & your skills:__ Be sure that you also have all of your needed digital devices in good working order and ready to succeed. Check your devices' video camera/microphone and make sure you know how to look as professional as possible (here is a great video to help you with that: **https://youtu.be/dkkdAsS6wCk**).

Bookmark your courses' homepage, the library homepage, and any other website you will be using regularly. Become familiar with your university's course management system such as Moodle, Canvas, or Blackboard. Make sure you clean up your laptop so that you have plenty of space for your new assignments and projects. Finally, clean up your email inbox so that you are as organized as possible to ensure that you don't miss important emails from your professor, the university administration, or fellow students.

Organizing Time: Simply put, you need to schedule important events so that you avoid being late, can properly prepare for them, and so that you don't forget them (this can be very costly on your grade point average). Use an online calendar and put in your class schedule as well as when all major events are due. Use your class syllabus to identify all important due dates and mark them in your calendar/planner.

Be specific as to when you will be studying for a test and working on a project. If you need even more reminders, a technique I sometimes use (for really important events/situations) is to schedule an email to be sent to my future self). If you use Gmail, there is a drop-down arrow on the "send" button that will allow you to schedule when the email is to be sent.

Put in other events such as appointments, working out, employment, and dedicated study time. In this way, you will be better able to manage your time and appropriately schedule other important events like going out with friends or other *fun activities*. These other *fun activities* are also important for your mental health but must be organized around your mission to succeed academically.

Always be realistic as you make your schedule. Make time for studying, as well as for eating, for exercise, and for breaks. Consistently following your schedule will help you develop discipline and will help you avoid procrastination. Be sure to check your calendar every morning and adjust when needed – remember that you are always in control.

***Great tools for this are:** Google Calendar and Microsoft Calendar. Make sure it is all synched with your cellphone and set reminders/alarms.

***Work to properly estimate how long it takes you to accomplish tasks:** In order to have an effective schedule, you need to properly estimate how long it will take to accomplish different tasks. Keep track of how long it takes you to read different chapters from different subjects (a chapter in a science book might take a different amount of time than reading a chapter from an English book). Be realistic with estimating the time needed for study/reading within your schedule.

***Do not multi-task!** We all think we can do it, but all that happens is that your performance suffers. Sure, take breaks when needed (that is when you can minimally check your phone), but do NOT think that you can effectively study and Facebook/Tik Tok/Instagram/etc. at the same time. Multi-book author, learning researcher, and CEO of an educational technology company, Olav Schewe, warns students that multitasking "is inefficient and ineffective, since the constant switching between tasks leads to loss of accuracy and a slowdown in speed" (2018, p. 11).

This is a hard lesson that I have learned and a hard lesson that my students have learned and one that they express is a vital element to grasp as soon as possible to improve their focus and lower stress. Although we all think we are saving time when multitasking, we are often doing both things slower and less effectively resulting in having to study longer.

***Avoid Time Drainers:** You need to personally identify anything within your daily routine that takes excessive amounts of time from your studying and find ways to eliminate it or at least minimize it. Be honest with yourself. Are you watching too much TV, YouTube, Netflix, and/or Tik Tok videos online? Are you playing too many videogames on your PlayStation, X-Box, VR headset, cellphone, etc.? Are you spending too much of your time on social media?

None of these things are bad in and of themselves, the problem comes when these things become a priority instead of your educational mission. View study time and homework as extremely important to a point that it may, at times, require you to cut into your other non-mission-critical activities. Treat these other activities as rewards for accomplishing your primary educational mission. Master delayed gratification. Again, remember that you are in control of these other activities, they are not in control of you.

Superpower #3: PARTICIPATE

– Super Presence Powers

Description: Be an active member of the class learning community. Ask and answer questions and be an active part of class discussions (be an active learner).

Importance: Research shows that students who actively participate in class are better able to recall information learned in class. Professors from the University of Toronto, in researching 735 college students' academic performance, found that "The degree to which students participated was positively associated with performance on formal exams" (Riggs, et al., 2020, p. 1). Similarly, educational, and psychological researchers Regan Gurung and Beth Schwartz, in their book *Optimizing Teaching and Learning: Practicing Pedagogical Research*, directly stated that:

> Students who are engaged allow themselves to be involved and a part of the class. When a student is engaged, he or she is more apt to study and participate in class and therefore be successful with their college careers. Correspondingly, increasing engagement is an important part of optimizing learning. (2009, p. 95)

Students who can harness this superpower and actively participate and engage (raising your hand, taking part in discussions) in class also tend to become part of the community of learning and are better able to understand the information presented.

Note that when you ask questions in class you are probably asking a question that others similarly have but are too timid to ask. By being a hero and having the courage to ask, you are helping yourself and others get clarification to properly learn.

Explanation: Professors and Learning science researchers have discovered what seems obvious but must be continually reiterated, your brain is much more active when you are fully engaged in the instruction which leads to better understanding and learning (Gurung & Schwartz, 2009).

The way to maximize your engagement is to fully participate by asking questions, taking good notes, doing the readings or assigned problems, answering questions completely, participating in the online forums, and being part of any class discussion (actively contribute, don't just passively listen).

Being part of the learning community means that you are actively trying to help not only yourself but others in the learning process as well.

Look at the difference in the following brain scan images done by Stanford University psychology department researchers Steven W. Cole, Daniel J. Yoo, and Brian Knutson when comparing someone passively observing (left) versus actively involved (right) in the learning process. Focus on the different portions of the brain and how they are either active/engaged or completely inactive/not engaged (2012).

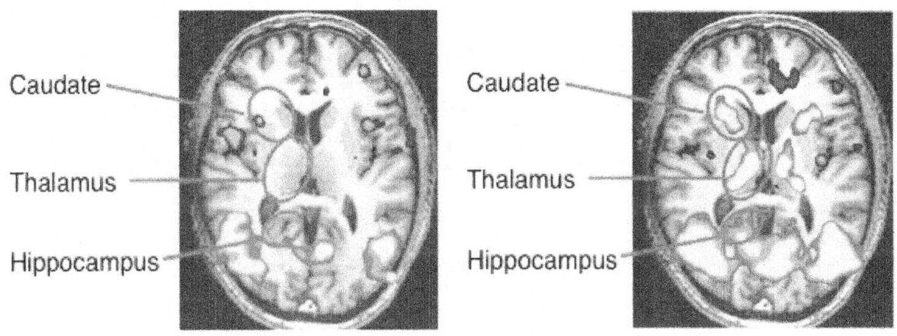

Passively Observing (left) vs. Actively Involved (right)
– image credit: Stanford University

Notice how the caudate (responsible for learning and processing memories), thalamus (responsible for processing and filtering all sensory information, except for smell), and the hippocampus (responsible for converting short term memories into long term memories) portions of the brain are much more active and engaged when someone is actively involved in doing/learning.

Hopefully, this stresses the overall point and convinces you of the vital importance of being fully active in class in order to maximize your learning. By doing things like answering class forum questions (and responding to others' posts), setting up study groups, and fully participating in class, you model proper academic behavior, gain additional connection to the content, and therefore learn the material at a much deeper level.

Georgetown University Professor Cal Newport, in his book *How to Win at College,* goes so far as to state "Make sure that you always ask at least one question at every lecture" (2005, p. 46). This is perfect advice in that it will help you stay focused, understand the material better, and help the professor see you in a positive light. This is also a powerful way to fully take control of your own learning and your own destiny.

***Contribute:** Seek additional ways to participate in and outside of class. If there happen to be extra credit assignments available, do it (even if you don't need the extra points). If there is an optional quiz or a quiz that you can retake if you want, do it to gain skills mastery. If there is an essay competition going on, participate. If there is any other type of academic contest, submit something. Yes, it would be great to win, but you also gain so much from failure as well as just going through the process of participating.

Reflect and learn from all of your endeavors (this builds greater understanding, persistence, and resilience).

***Realize and Remember that you Are in Control**: Additional brain scan research has shown that people who physically take control of their learning remember the content better (Voss, et al., 2011). You are the one deciding when to learn and how to learn, you are in control and will determine your own level of success. Chose to participate and don't let anything stand in the way of learning the material.

Superpower #4: BE MOTIVATED AND RESILIENT – *Super Willpower*

Description: Being motivated (excited, interested, and focused) on the learning task at hand, regardless of other events or situations that are occurring; able to recover from negative events and endure (resilience).

Importance: Becoming and staying motivated will help you to go to class and pay attention which will then help you learn and succeed academically. Having resiliency means that even though negative situations may occur (such as sickness, the death of a loved one, etc.) you will be able to quickly bounce back (recover) and accomplish your learning mission. A motivated and resilient mind translates into having super willpower which is one of the strongest superpowers that you must develop.

Explanation: As a professor, I work hard to motivate my students by using good instructional techniques and informing students of the relevance of what we are studying. Unfortunately, not all instructors will be like this, and you might find yourself in a boring lecture. You must always work to become and stay self-motivated to learn.

Realize that boredom is the death nail of learning as identified by instructional researchers Pekrun, Goetz, Frenzel, Barchfeld, and Perry, when analyzing the results of an Achievement Emotions Questionnaire given to 395 university students (2011). Influential American educational psychologist, John Keller, said it best when describing his model of motivation: if you become bored you will lose focus and not pay attention; if you aren't paying attention, then you will not learn (Keller, 1987).

Ways to be Self-Motivated and Resilient:

> **Have a Growth Mindset:** World-renowned researcher, professor, and author Carol Dweck, identified a *growth mindset* as meaning that you realize that you can indeed improve your intelligence/capabilities and that when problems or difficulties occur, they are viewed as challenges to overcome, not reasons to quit (2017). This ties in with the aspect of grit (persevering): enduring and pushing yourself to succeed.
>
> Avoid having a *fixed mindset* which means that you do not believe that you can improve and that you become averse to anything that challenges you or becomes difficult (Dweck, 2017). Having a growth mindset is one of the most powerful ways to stay motivated and achieve resiliency.

Dweck, when highlighting the power of a growth mindset to maintain motivating, expressed students' actual comments who had developed a strong growth mindset:

Instead of losing their motivation when the course got dry or difficult, they said: "I maintained my interest in the material." "I stayed positive about taking chemistry." "I kept myself motivated to study." Even if they thought the textbook was boring or the instructor was a stiff, they didn't let their motivation evaporate. That just made it all the more important to motivate themselves. (2017, p. 60)

Identify both the short-term and long-term relevancy of what you are studying. Yes, you want to do well to get an "A+" in this class (short-term), but how will this help you in the long run? Perhaps this is key material for your next class, or you are learning techniques (such as proper APA citation) that you will need to use again and again in future classes. Always identify and focus on relevancy - stay motivated.

This ties in with having both **short-term and long-term goals** to have something to accomplish and look forward to. Just be sure to always make your goals S.M.A.R.T goals (Specific, Measurable, Achievable, Relevant, Timely) – as developed by productivity business expert Doran (1981). See the included worksheet towards the end of this book for additional S.M.A.R.T goals guidance.

Break Everything into Manageable Chunks: It can become easy to get overwhelmed and stressed out when given large assignments. To overcome this, simply look at the assignment as regular sections that need to be done then put together. As an example, a big term paper isn't a large monster, it just requires going through the 7 Step Writing Process: Choose a Topic, Brainstorm, Outline, Draft, Get Feedback, Revise, Proofread.

> *Additional information on the 7 Step Writing Process presented later in this book.

In the same way, don't view a big test as something that you will have to study for many hours, all night for the day/night before. Instead view it as something that requires you to study and quiz yourself on early on for a shorter amount of time, but on a regular basis. Organize your time so that you can study multiple days/weeks before the test so that it is conducted in practical chunks. In this way, big assignments and tests will seem much more manageable and will be much easier to accomplish.

Avoid Catastrophizing: Many students become overly anxious and stressed out because they overthink a situation and/or event. As an example, a lot of students avoid participating in class because they are catastrophizing what might occur. They think "I might say something wrong in class, this will make my instructor think I'm stupid and all the other students will laugh at me, I'll get a bad grade, and then I'll get kicked out of college." The reality is of course much different.

The best way to overcome catastrophizing is to not only think about the worst outcome but also the best outcome ("my instructor will think I'm a genius and everyone will applaud"), and finally think about the most likely outcome ("I will give a good answer which the instructor will appreciate, and my answer will help move the class/discussion along"). If you are still worried about a negative outcome, take the necessary steps (taking notes, studying, being prepared) in order to stay motivated and resilient which will result in your success.

Make Your Bed: It may sound silly, but there is actually a powerful mental invigoration that occurs when you successfully make your bed first thing in the morning. By doing so you are starting your day by accomplishing something. Now you can mentally tell yourself that you have just succeeded in a small thing which means that you can also succeed in bigger things. You are ready for a continued pattern of success. By constantly doing this you are also building discipline. This discipline can now be applied in the development of your other superpowers.

This concept of motivation and discipline, starting from simply making your bed in the morning, is also eloquently expressed by retired United States Navy four-star admiral William Harry McRaven, during an impactful commencement speech at the University of Texas, at Austin. The admiral describes ten powerful lessons he learned in Navy Seal training, one of which was the impact of simply making your bed in the morning (**https://youtu.be/pxBQLFLei70**).

Reflect: In a similar way, you need to periodically stop and *reflect* on all your accomplishments. Reflect on all the tests you've passed, the projects you've completed, the books you've read, and the people you have helped. You have already come a long way and will go on to do even bigger and better things. You have already developed perseverance / grit in order to get where you are now. Be proud of that and know that you can continue to do so much more. I believe in you, and you must believe in yourself as well.

Don't be a Hermit: Although you might think that the best way to succeed as a student is to do nothing else but go to class and study, you need to do other things. Find clubs or organizations that are fun and interesting. Try new things to see if you might find joy in doing them. You need to find outlets for your pent-up energy as well as find ways to relax and enjoy your leisure time. Just remember that although it is important for overall mental wellbeing, it needs to be balanced with your other academic responsibilities. Be sure to be organized and schedule all your time wisely.

Help Others: This one might seem weird, but by helping others understand and learn the material, you actually greatly help yourself in two distinct ways: you gain a deeper understanding of the material, and you increase your self-esteem / spiritual wellbeing by helping someone else succeed. Be an active member of a learning community/study group so that you can help others.

Teaching others requires you to know at a higher level and the act of vocalizing the instructional material will help you recreate additional neural connections to the learning material (Gurung & Schwartz, 2009). All of this helps to keep you motivated/focused and that is what a good Super Student hero would do.

***Avoid Procrastination:** Be very wary of *procrastination* and fully realize that it is the "kryptonite" to your powers! You need to avoid procrastination in that it can actually counteract your superpowers. If you ever catch yourself procrastinating (wanting to be lazy, putting things off like assignments/test-studying to the last second), stop and review the previously stated keys to being self-motivating.

You must always be honest with yourself, reflect, and realize when you are putting things off for unwarranted reasons. When you feel the urge and powerful desire to procrastinate, remind yourself of your very first superpower (*BE YOUR FUTURE BEST FRIEND*) and put a stop to your procrastination. Remember, only you are in charge of your destiny, and we are all counting on you.

***A Note About Online Learning:** Let go of any negative feelings you might have about online learning in that it won't help you in being a Super Student. Research has repeatedly shown that it isn't the delivery mechanism that determines whether a class is good or bad; a face-to-face course isn't better than an online course just because it is conducted face-to-face (Cavanaugh & Jacquemin, 2015; Driscoll, Jicha, et al., 2012; White, McGowan, & McDonald, 2019).

I have taken plenty of great face-to-face courses, just like I've taken plenty of great online courses. In the same breath, I must state that I've taken some bad face-to-face courses, as well as bad online courses. It is the instructor and his/her instructional techniques that make the difference.

Give your instructor a chance, regardless of the instructional delivery method. Use the other superpowers provided within this book and succeed no matter what.

Although it might seem hard to see online learning as a privilege (especially for those who were forced to learn online due to the Coronavirus) it is actually a powerful privilege that we should fully realize.

Consider if the pandemic had happened just 25 years ago when the internet was just starting to be known. Most universities would have simply shut down and students would have had their educational progress put on pause for a year or more, forgetting a lot and not being able to properly advance. Thanks to the technological marvel that is the internet, we can continue to go through courses, learn, and develop our educational capabilities.

Consider the way that online learning has been an essential saving element for thousands of other students in the not-too-distant past. Within the last few decades, there have been multiple natural disasters, wars, and other pandemics that devastated different regions around the world; however, students were still able to successfully continue with their education thanks to online learning (Schroeder, 2021).

Being grateful for the technology that we are privileged to have at our fingertips is an important aspect to accept to have a positive mindset and be as resilient as possible.

***Adult Learner Core Principles:** If you are an Adult Learner, which means you are either physically older than many in your class (generally over 22) or you have many additional responsibilities that typically come from being an adult (living with a spouse, raising kids, taking care of a parent, and/or a full-time job), realize some other aspects of your learning that might be affecting your motivation.

Highly regarded education and adult learning professors and researchers, Malcolm Knowles, Elwood F. Holton, and Richard A. Swanson developed six core adult learning principles that generally encompass adults learners' attitudes/orientations: 1) Learner's Need to Know (a desire to understand the why, what, and how, as well as a need for greater engagement in learning, 2) Self-Concept of the Learner (a desire to be more self-directing), 3) Prior Experience of the Learner (having prior experience recognized and valued), 4) Readiness to Learn (a need to see the relevance and possible additional assistance), 5) Orientation to Learning (a preference for problem-solving), 6) Motivation to Learn (more internal motivation with a need for current relevancy), (Knowles, Holton, & Swanson, 2005).

Tactically, talk to your instructor if these aspects are not being met in your class. If need be, seek to address these issues on your own through realization and direct action like asking questions, seeking additional help, and finding your own personal motivations.

An infographic on these core adult learning principles is provided towards the back of this book to aid in your understanding and for your convenience.

Superpower #5: USE THE LIBRARY – *Super Intelligence Powers*

Description: Go to and fully use your school's library. Understand that it is much, much more than just a place to go and check out books.

Importance: The university library is the heart of the university and as such offers a wealth of resources. Mastering these resources will give you a new superpower that can help ensure that you will succeed in all of your academic pursuits. Yes, there are needed books there, but there are also tons of other resources there such as free wi-fi, meeting rooms, and a wealth of knowledgeable people there ready to help you succeed.

Explanation: Research has shown that students who spend a large amount of time in the school's library tend to be more academically successful (Brown, & Malenfant, 2017; Soria, 2013). This of course is a correlation, not necessarily a causation, but it is important to understand why academically successful students are spending time in the library.

One big benefit of modern libraries is that they typically offer an excellent place to study. It is quiet (find the quiet place that works best for you), generally has fewer distractions than your room at home, offers free wi-fi, is academically inspirational, has good seating, and offers special areas for group work (conference rooms).

Additionally, libraries offer access to not just physical books, but e-books, subscription-only research databases, and audio/video resources as well. Yet often one of the most under-utilized resources available at the library are the Liberians and staff. These trained professionals can help you with proper citation, can assist you in finding excellent sources of information, and are knowledgeable in virtually all areas. This means they can help you answer your assignment questions or help you find out the best place to find the answer, whether that is in a physical book or online.

> ***Online Resource:** Be sure to realize that the library is also a powerful resource when you are away from the physical library building itself. You might be away from the library due to illness, you could be an online-only student, or lock-down quarantine measures might be ongoing. Many university libraries provide online book reservations, access to online materials, and even advanced access to special materials with a school login.
>
> A great service offered by the University where I work at is online chat, where they can answer any question students (as well instructors and staff) might have live through the internet, regardless of where they might be, either on campus or away.

Consistently spending time in the library is a superpower that will also help develop your scholarly culture. A culture where you see and understand the importance of learning, of improving, and of becoming a life-long learner.

By developing this type of learning mindset from the library, you will also have greater intrinsic motivation by better cherishing knowledge and the process of obtaining it (a love of learning for the sake of learning itself).

Superpower #6: STUDY PROPERLY (distributed practice+)

– Super Mind-Control Powers

Description: Use appropriate studying techniques such as the concept of repeated quizzing/testing when learning the course material.

Importance: By using better studying techniques you will save time and improve your assignment and test scores. This will increase your overall grade and give you more time for other activities.

Explanation: Although there are many aspects to effective studying, learning of the material, the most powerful tool (superpower) available for you for this is the process of distributed practice, specifically through active repeated testing.

Known by several names and concepts (testing effect, retrieval practice, active study, repeated retrieval effect), *distributed practice* has been shown to be extremely effective in helping students score well on exams across multiple subjects, grade levels, and via both online and face-to-face learning (Brown, et al., 2014; Jost, 2021; Oakley & Schewe, 2017).

The best way to learn and retain the information is through this process of repeated testing. By going through this process of testing/quizzing after you have sat through a class and/or read the material, you will lessen (interrupt) forgetting; in other words, it will help you to NOT forget what you have learned. For full (deep) learning when conducting repeated testing, be sure to be able to *identify, define, be able to use it in a sentence/paragraph, identify differences/similarities between concepts*, and *apply the info being learned in new ways.*

Many times, textbooks will offer built-in quizzes or study questions, use those to repeatedly quiz/test yourself in order to prepare for graded tests/quizzes in that this technique is much more effective than just rereading and highlighting the text or your notes (Brown, et al., 2014). If practice tests/quizzes/study questions aren't available, then create them yourself (you could even exchange made-up questions with other students for more variation).

The key with this technique is repeated spaced out practice to improve memory of the learned material. Do not try to cram all of your practice testing/quizzing on the night before the test; again, the key is repeated spaced out practice. The spacing of your repeated practice/testing is dependent on the time frame you have from when you were first exposed to the material to when you will be evaluated. The general recommendation is to go no more than one week in between your own self-practice testing (Brown, et al., 2014).

The key takeaway here is that **you will have a greatly enhanced capability (superpower) to learn faster and more deeply by regularly quizzing/testing yourself** as opposed to just rereading the material (the act of being tested is the key).

There are many ways to test quiz yourself such as writing out your own quiz/test, making physical flashcards, using PowerPoint, or using cellphone apps such as:

AnkiApp: cross-platform mobile/desktop flashcard app: **https://www.ankiapp.com**

Brainscape: cross-platform mobile/desktop flashcard app: **https://www.brainscape.com**

Note-Taking is Important – Be Sure to do it the Right Way: Don't write everything down, just note the key concepts and draw figures and processes whenever possible. In addition to capturing information for later study, note-taking also helps with staying focused and paying attention (the key is to pay attention and ask questions – don't let the act of note-taking distract you from that). Compare your notes with others and review your notes periodically to gain the benefits of the repeated retrieval effect.

Taking notes by hand or on a laptop are both beneficial but use what works best for you.
If having your laptop open is too distracting since it allows for access to the Internet and all your apps, then consider temporarily turning your wi-fi off or taking hand-written notes. Professors and educational/psychology researchers from the University of Iowa stated that "Writing down what the instructor is saying in class essentially 'forces' students to pay closer attention to what is being said, and 'reinforces' their retention (memory) of what has been said" (Cuseo, Fecas, & Thompson, 2010, p. 2).

***Memorization:** don't try to memorize everything, especially since everything can be Googled. Do work on memorizing key concepts, very important fundamental data, in that it will save you time and allow for a deeper understanding of more advanced concepts. Use mnemonics (memory aids) like loci, gestures, and acronyms to help you memorize needed information, but don't ever assume that others will know that acronym (such as when writing out an essay or short answer).

Visualize and make a picture whenever possible. Research has shown again and again that it is easier to memorize a concrete image rather than an abstract concept (Hockley, 2008; Paivio, et al., 1968).

> – Here is another powerful bonus of repeated practice (repeated testing): by repeatedly quizzing/testing yourself on the instructional content, you will start to memorize the content *without even trying*!

***Read for Comprehension, Not Speed:** I recommend taking notes on your reading, summarize, make connections, and try to come up with good questions that you would ask if you were the professor (use this as part of your repeated testing/practice study). Draw pictures/diagrams/charts whenever possible to make the text more graphical, which makes the material easier to remember and understand.

Reading in this way will save you time and energy in the long run. After your reading always reflect on what were the main concepts and how it relates to the rest of the course.

***Make Connections:** A powerful way to achieve deep learning and to help you remember learned material is by making connections to what is being learned in multiple ways. Learning scientists and professors/teachers Barbara Oakley, Terry Sejnowski, Alistair McConville, in their bestselling book *Learning to Learn*, strongly recommends making as many connections as you can between ideas (how does this relate to that, how does this apply to the real world, how is this personally relevant) as well as learning the material through multiple means such as reading, listening, and watching videos (2018).

The different learning modalities aid in making additional connections to the instructional content. – The more connections (neural web of connectivity) you have to the material, the deeper the learning and the easier it will be to retrieve (remember). Consider writing out mind maps as well, to physically see how the information is connected.

***Test-Taking Tips:**

- Take properly spaced practice tests beforehand
- Put your name and required info at the top of the test (for written tests)
- Read each question carefully (twice)
- Answer the entire question, not just the first part (many tests ask two-part questions that often aren't fully addressed = lost points)

- Keep track of time and move on if you become stuck on a particular question (come back to it later)
- Review all your answers (make sure everything is in the right order and you have gone back to any question you skipped or didn't finish)
- After the test, reflect by conducting an Educational After Actions Review (AAR):

  The AAR is an effective U.S. Army technique to help you review an event and improve (Anders, 2020). Ask yourself these simple questions:

  - What went right for me during this test?
  - What went wrong for me during this test?
  - How can I do things better next time?

    Identify things like did you take good, helpful notes in class, did you spend enough time studying alone, did you study the right material, were the study groups you attended beneficial, did you get enough sleep, etc.

  See the Educational After Actions Review worksheet in the back of the book for more guidance.

***Physically Studying:** Be honest with yourself and realize that you will be able to focus better and be more effective if you are studying in a quiet place that doesn't have distractions. The library is usually that place but be sure it is the quiet areas of the library. If it is too busy, then find another area that is quiet and will allow you to focus.

Generally, you are better off studying by yourself with some study group time when needed or help with a group project. Again, reflect and study in the most effective way for you to ensure success.

***Breaks are Important Too:** A great technique for including breaks is the Pomodoro Technique (Cirillo, 2006). With this simple, but effective technique, you eliminate all distractors (put your phone on airplane mode/wi-fi off, etc.) and dutifully work/study for 25 minutes and then take a 5-minute break. I use a slightly modified version when I really need to get things done.

I work/study for 30 minutes, then take 2 minutes to check my phone (for messages/emails), then I take a purposeful break for 8 minutes. By *purposeful break* I mean go for walk, talk to family/friends in person, or close my eyes and just relax. The key to the *purposeful break* is to take a break from your screen (laptop/cellphone/tablet).

As an example of the merits of this, research conducted on nurses found a positive benefit on reported feelings of being "burn-out" when they were able to take periodic walking breaks in hospital gardens (Cordoza, et al., 2018).

Taking a walk during your break will greatly help by giving you some time away from your screen, exposing you to fresh air, and getting the blood moving from the physical exercise.

You can use the timer/alarm on your cellphone to do the Pomodoro Technique with purposeful breaks or you can use other timing tools such as:

Pomodor (Web based App):
https://pomodor.app/timer

Forest (IOS or Android App):
https://www.forestapp.cc

***Difficulty is Actually Good:** Remember to have a growth mindset and view difficulty simply as challenges to overcome. Also, remember that difficulty can be beneficial, "difficulty is a crucial part of learning, errors are natural and to be expected, and practice helps" (Brown, et al., 2014, p. 47). Difficulty and challenges actually mean that your brain is working and forming new connections.

***Use of Study Music:** Be careful when choosing to have music playing in the background while studying in that many studies have not shown positive effects and some have even found negative effects due to possible distraction (de la Mora Velasco, E., & Hirumi, A., 2020; Schellenberg, 2006).

Yet some of us do enjoy listening to background music at times when studying and some research indicates there may be some benefit for some students (Angel, et al. 2010; Schellenberg, & Weiss, 2013; Shih, et al., 2021). It seems that different music seems to affect different people in different ways. In general, if you are going to play music, be sure it is relaxing, does not have vocals, and does not introduce distractions either through too fast of a beat, unexpected advertisements (such as through free streaming music), or evoking too strong of emotion (sadness, etc.).

The key is relaxing music, which can help motivate, focus, but not make you go to sleep or distract you from your studies. The key is to be reflective and honest with yourself as always. If the music is distracting you then don't listen to it in that it will detract from your studies.

Here is a link to some free relaxing study music that I put together for you:

> Version 1 (more classical):
> **https://youtu.be/3q0MRDSUEOo**
>
> Version 2 (more modern):
> **https://youtu.be/c0LVen2Z-ec**

***Writing:** Being able to write effectively is an extremely powerful capability that will help you in virtually every other subject you study. Improve your writing capabilities by writing as often as possible. Use tools like Grammarly (fully described a little later in this book), keep a journal or diary, and for essay creation, use the 7 Step Writing Process (infographic available toward the back of this book).

Follow the 7 Step Writing Process to create the best essays and to save time in its overall creation. Although some might think that it takes longer to go through the 7 steps, following each step will actually save you time in the long run, especially in that after developing an essay outline, the actual essay will practically write itself.

> **Academic Writing:** Remember key elements when doing academic writing. Write in the third person (he/she/it), be objective, avoid figurative language, be more formal, be precise (don't exaggerate or make extreme claims), and use proper citations.
>
> Be sure to check with your instructor(s) for their specific guidelines and follow the writing format and citation style for that class/subject.

***Increase Video Watch Speed:** When watching videos, especially online videos like YouTube, you can save time by going into the video settings and increasing the video playback or watch speed. If the speaker in the video is slow then this will bring them up to a better speed, if not then the information will be presented at a faster than usual rate. For this reason, it is vital that for you to effectively understand the information, you focus on the video. As stated earlier, multi-tasking does not work, and playing video faster will make things even worse **if you are not fully concentrating** on the presentation.

Similarly, if the speaker has a thick accent or the language used is your secondary language, then playing the video back slower (as well as using closed captions) might be a smart technique to better understand and retain the information.

***Create (Creation of Higher-Level Products):** During one of my Ph.D. courses, I became very anxious in that we were having to learn many different qualitative research aspects that were becoming hard for me (and the rest of the class) to differentiate and keep straight. I finally realized that what I needed was to make the content more visual; so, I created an infographic to help make the content more understandable and memorable.

By visualizing and creating the content in this different way, it made me *have to* engage with the content on a deeper level and create more advanced connections and relationships with the material.

I then decided to help my learning community and shared the infographic with the rest of class. They were extremely grateful and expressed how much it helped them as well. Creating infographics or other explanatory class products: graphics / charts / diagrams / mind maps are another powerful way to participate by helping yourself as well as others succeed.

This next section of this chapter deals with the + part of how to Study Properly

Use Bloom's Taxonomy: In a similar way to my suggestion of creating higher-level products to help you understand and learn the information presented, Dr. Justin Sung, former medical doctor and educator/social entrepreneur co-founder of iCanStudy, describes an excellent technique of using Bloom's Taxonomy to better study and learn information (iCanStudy, 2021).

Bloom's Revised Taxonomy (image on the next page) deals with different aspects of the cognitive domain (mental capability/knowledge) from lower complexity (bottom: *remember*) to the most complex (the top: *create*), (Krathwohl & Anderson, 2009).

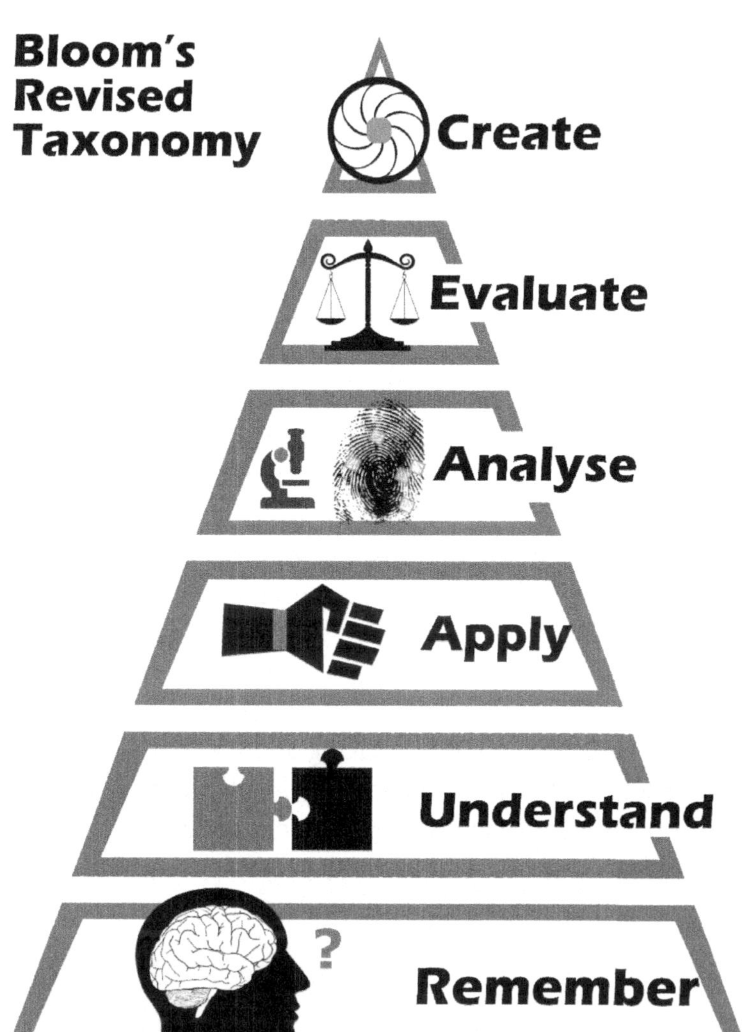

Bloom's Revised Taxonomy, original art by Brent A. Anders, derived from research conducted by Krathwohl & Anderson (2009)

Six different levels: 1. Remember (recognizing, identifying, memorizing), 2. Understand (interpreting, summarizing, explaining), 3. Apply (executing, implementing), 4. Analyze (differentiating, attributing), 5. Evaluate (checking, critiquing), and 6. Create (generating, producing).

The main aspect of Dr. Sung's recommendation deals with focusing one's studying/learning on upper levels of Bloom's Taxonomy (iCanStudy, 2021). The idea is that instead of starting on the lower levels (1. Remember and 2. Understand) you start on higher levels. In concentrating on these higher levels, your mind will automatically go through the lower levels of remembering and understanding as it applies, analyses, evaluates, and creates. **Using the higher levels of cognitive domains will save you time in studying and forces you to create enhanced relationships and relevancies equaling longer retention and better learning.**

As an example of this, Elon Musk, multi-disciplinary genius, entrepreneur, and world's richest man (Biography, 2021), in describing his own created private school: Ad Astra, explained that instead of teaching students about tools first and then moving on to more advanced topics, they start with an advanced task such as taking apart an engine (Castlefrank, 2018). Now students have enhanced motivation/relevancy in wanting to know about different tools (and build stronger associations/relationships) in order to accomplish the higher-level task.

It is important to realize that both distributed practice and the use of product creation/Bloom's Taxonomy are extremely beneficial when studying and learning. Realize that product creation/Bloom's Taxonomy can generally offer a greater level of benefit when studying more advanced (higher-level) material. Understand and use all the techniques described and find what works best for you and the material being learned.

Superpower #7: SEEK HELP

– Super Vision Powers

Description: Be able and willing to seek additional guidance and assistance when needed and through the proper channels (*even Superman and Wonder Woman would turn to the Justice League when they needed additional help – Thor and Ironman would turn to the rest of the Avengers as well*).

Importance: By knowing and being able to follow good help-seeking behaviors your ability to succeed academically will greatly improve. Additionally, seeking help in the right way will help save you time and prevent you from harming your grades. Get the help you need early so you can see the right way to accomplish the assignment and understand the material.

Explanation: To begin with, some students feel shy or somehow believe that they should not seek help when they don't understand the assignment or the information presented. Remember the related superpower of *Participation* which was already discussed.

Seeking help is a powerful life skill that you need to have in order to succeed. Your professor wants you to ask questions and seek help. Ask your question in class if others might benefit. If not, see if the professor is available after class or schedule office hours with him/her.

> ***Note:** be sure to check the syllabus for your class. Nothing aggravates a professor more than answering a question that is clearly stated in the syllabus.

Having talked and worked with hundreds of professors, they truly do want to talk to you and are happy to answer your questions either in person, through web-conferencing (like Zoom), or via email. If asking a question via email, be professional (formal with proper etiquette/netiquette), state who you are, what class/section you are in, and ask your question as clearly as possible.

Use this power and be willing to seek help when needed. Seek help earlier, before it becomes a much bigger problem and affects your grades.

Other Great Places to Get Help:

Library: Remember that the library not only has great information, but they also have very knowledgeable staff that want to help you and see you succeed. They can provide great assistance in a variety of topics as well as help you find great online help as well.

Study Groups: If you are having ongoing issues with class, a study group might be a great way for you to learn from your peers as all of you progress through the class. The group (as a whole) can also pose additional questions to the instructor if needed.

Class Learning Community: Many courses add an online forum where students can pose questions to the class and other students and/or the professor can answer. Similarly, many times, students create a private Facebook group (or something similar) where students can privately discuss and ask questions amongst themselves about the course. This might be a good resource to see if someone has answered your question(s).

Student Success Center (Academic Support Services): Many universities have a dedicated office such as a Student Success Center that functions to help students overcome issues in their academic process. They might offer help with your writing capabilities or offer tutoring to help you improve math or other sciences. Check with what is available and use this excellent resource whenever you need help.

Counseling Services: At times, any of us might need additional assistance to help us overcome issues (either academic or other, more personal issues). Know that going to counseling services is a sign of strength, not weakness. Use this service to your advantage so that you can improve and continue, so that you can succeed in all your courses. – Remember to also maintain your needed support network of family and friends so that all of you can lean on each other during hardships.

Online Resources: Some great, free, additional online resources are available to help you succeed:

Grammarly: Highly recommended tool (I used it when writing this book) to assist with composition - grammar editing: **https://www.grammarly.com**

Khan Academy: Provides lots of useful assistance review (at all levels), especially with STEM (sciences) subjects. This resource also provides gamification components that increase motivation and persistance: **https://www.khanacademy.org**

Evernote: Effective online notes and to-do list creator, usable/synched across multiple devices: **https://evernote.com**

GoConqr: Online tool to create mind maps (visual concept connector), flashcards, quizzes, flowcharts, and more: **https://www.goconqr.com**

***Avoid Plagiarism/Cheating:** Note that all these help-seeking methods offer help, but they don't simply give you all the answers or do the work for you; that would be unethical, meaning cheating, which equals plagiarism.

You must avoid plagiarism at all costs in that it will prevent you from fully learning the material and once caught will result in negative academic consequences.

Address all understanding and learning issues as early as possible so that they don't create situations where you feel this extremely risky and self-defeating behavior seems like a good idea.

Having worked in many different countries with different cultures, plagiarism can sometimes be viewed as not that important. You need to understand that the world is becoming smaller, and your capabilities are becoming more and more important. To be competitive in this global economy you don't just need a degree, you need a real education, a developed ability to learn, and a life-long learning attitude. A good education comes from properly studying and doing the work, not from copying or being dishonest in your academic journey.

A *New York Times* quote from Laszlo Bock, the senior vice president of people operations for Google poignantly expresses the need to be a good learner when talking about the type of people they are looking to hire, “For every job, though, the No. 1 thing we look for is general cognitive ability, and it’s not I.Q. It’s learning ability” (Friedman, 2014).

Be the Super Student and hero that you are truly meant to be. Do the right thing, learn the material, continue to improve your ability to learn, set the example for others, and avoid plagiarism.

Superpower #8: EXERCISE, NUTRITION, and SLEEP

– Super Strength Powers

Description: Ensure that in addition to your academic pursuits you are being physically active, eating well, and getting appropriate rest.

Importance: Research has shown that all three of these components (exercise, nutrition, and sleep) need to be properly addressed in order to learn more effectively (Doherty, et al. 2019; Van Praag, 2009). Additionally, by exercising, eating well, and getting good sleep, energy levels will increase and motivation to continue studying and learning will be enhanced as well (Oakley, et al., 2018).

Explanation: This superpower is essential to understand and master. Realize that all three of these components (exercise, nutrition, and sleep) are equally as vital for your academic success and general health as well.

EXERCISE: It might seem counterintuitive, but research has shown that regular exercise gives you more energy (Puetz, et al., 2006; Westcott, 2012); energy that you can use to stay motivated and complete your studies. The other powerful aspect to exercise is that it helps to build new neurons which helps you to learn new material and make better connections (Oakley, et al., 2018; Van Praag, 2009).

Regularly exercise 3 to 5 times per week and seek to do a mixture of resistance training (bodyweight, resistance bands, and/or actual weights) and cardio (running, biking, aerobics, etc.). This book isn't meant to be a fitness book, but in general, work out for 30 minutes to an hour each time for optimal health and learning benefits. Use good form and don't overdo it so that you can avoid injuries.

Schedule your workouts so that you can consistently gain all the advantages of regular workouts (aiding in building new neurons, improved energy/motivation, reduced stress, enhanced fitness levels, aid in managing bodyfat levels, and even getting a better night's rest).

> ***Yoga is Highly Recommended:** In addition to regular resistance/cardio workouts I also highly recommend yoga/stretching. I try and do about 12 to 20 minutes of yoga every morning to start the day off right. But, if you don't have that kind of time at least do my specially made 4-minute full-body yoga routine. It is super-fast and effective in helping to wake you up and get your entire body and mind ready for the day head.

See the 4-Minute Full Body Yoga routine towards the end of the book.

***10,000 Steps:** I also greatly recommend that everyone try and get 10,000 steps spread throughout the day. This is vital to avoid the dangers of a sedentary lifestyle that easily occurs for those of us that work in an office all day or spend a lot of time studying. Try to walk a bit in the morning, walk a little after every meal, and walk (especially outside) when taking a purposeful break.

Even if you can't go anywhere because you have a sweet spot at the library, get up and walk in-place so that you get the blood moving and gain the many researched benefits of getting your 10,000 steps in (Broaddus, et al., 2019; Stapp & Prior, 2018). Most cellphones have a built-in step counter, or you can download a free one from the internet.

***Don't Be Embarrassed:** If someone comes up to you and says:

> *"Hey, why are you walking in-place like that, this is the library."*

Don't feel embarrassed. Instead, feel good; use it as an opportunity to help them and say:

> "I'm getting the blood flowing to avoid the dangers of being sedentary and to gain the learning benefits of exercising. I read about it in this great book called *How to Be a Super Student: Based on Science and Experience*, available at Amazon."

NUTRITION: Eating a healthy balanced diet is another vital component that will directly assist you in your learning efforts. Professor and neural/learning science researcher from the Harvard University Extension School, Tracey Noel Tokuhama-Espinosa, explains that "Good eating habits contribute to learning, and poor eating habits detract from the brain's ability to maximize its learning potential" (2011, p. 124). She also expresses how the survival of newly created brain cells can be negatively affected by poor nutritional choices. Tokuhama-Espinosa's research has also found a link between poor nutrition and exacerbation of learning problems (2011, p. 125).

For better nourishment and to gain the learning benefits of good nutrition, eat a balanced diet that has good fats, proteins, and carbs. Eat as natural as possible (whole foods, lean meats, fresh vegetables, and fruits) and consciously work to avoid processed foods (chips, white bread, French fries, processed meats) and high-sugar foods (soda/pop, candy, & chocolate bars).

> **Avoid Energy Drinks:** To begin with they are nutritionally horrible for you; often being highly processed, having high sugar, and excessive amounts of stimulants. Additionally, they can be addictive and have also been negatively associated with learning. Kinesiology and Health Education researchers / professors Sara Champlin, Keryn Pasch, and Cheryl Perry, from the University of Texas, Austin, in a study on 844 freshman students found that "...greater energy drink consumption is associated with a lower GPA, even after controlling for potential confounding variables" (2016, p. 1). – *GPA (Grade Point Average)*

Be a Prepper: Reflect, be realistic, and prepare when it comes to good nutrition. If you are going to be at school all day or are planning to head to the library for several hours, then you will get hungry. What are you going to do when that happens?

Prepare by either making good nutritional meals to take with you or taking time to survey the available food venues in the area to identify easily and quickly accessible food that is affordable and highly nutritious.

Remember and be realistic in that if you get hungry while at school/studying, most people's first impulse is to just get a quick and cheap (sugary) snack from the vending machine or nearby store. Avoid this by prepping ahead of time.

Super Snack: My main snack/meal (that I prepare at home ahead of time) if I think I might be at work or studying a long time consists of two or three slices of hard cheese, a handful of walnuts, almonds, & raisins, and one or two small apples. This is a great snack/meal in that it is very natural, has some good fats, proteins, & carbs, and is packed with nutrients.

SLEEP: Treat sleep as part of your studying process. Sleep is a key component to learning in that "...brain-links solidify when you are sleeping!... During sleep, the brain rehearses what it has learned during the day" (Oakley, et al., 2018, p. 77).

To put it another way, I really like the colorful and visual language of the author, Stephen Covey, of one of my favorite books *The Seven Habits of Highly Effective People*, in addressing the importance of sleep when talking about the crucial balance of being productive and managing your own health:

> It's a principle you can see validated in your own life when you burn the candle at both ends to get more golden eggs and wind up sick or exhausted, unable to produce any at all; or when you get a good night's sleep and wake up ready to produce throughout the day. (p. 57)

Research indicates that the optimal level of sleep is between 7 to 9 hours for college students with key factors of consistency in bedtimes (regularly going to sleep at the same time) and quality of sleep, resulting in better academic performance (Pilcher, et al., 1997; Vedaa, et al., 2019).

Based on my experience, what other students have shared with me, and information from sleepadvisor.org, sleep.org, healthysleep.med.harvard.edu, and www.mayoclinic.org, to maximize the quality of your sleep and therefore enhance your learning, mood, and even motivation, follow a specific schedule for when you are to go to sleep as much as possible, wear loose, comfortable clothing as your sleeping garments, make your sleeping area as dark (wear a sleep mask if necessary) and quiet as you can, and try to keep the temperature cool, between 60-72 degrees (15-22 degrees Celsius).

Other things that can also help you have higher quality sleep are avoiding looking at your laptop/cell phone 30 minutes before you go to sleep, consuming a healthy balanced diet throughout the day, exercising regularly (but not within 90 minutes of bedtime), getting some sunlight exposure (no more than 30 minutes at a time), and avoiding caffeine, alcohol, and smoking as much as possible, especially 4 hours before bedtime.

If you are still having problems going to sleep, here are some tips I've learned in the military and through trial and error in my own educational pursuits:

- **Ensure that your nose is not stuffy**. Blow your nose and/or adjust your pillow. Not being able to breathe properly through your nose is often the biggest thing keeping people awake. If needed, use a neti-pot to help clear your nasal passageways.
- **Take a warm shower**. The calming effect that a warm shower provides often helps one relax and will get you to sleep faster.
- **Read an interesting informational book** (one that isn't too stimulating). This will start to make you tired and more ready to go to sleep. *Avoid reading off of a screen at night unless it is a digital ink e-book *(more info on the negative sleep effect of screens presented later).*
- *Although sleeping with socks on is uncomfortable for me, my wife and many others

(especially females) find that sleeping with warm socks on helps them sleep.

- **Make a To-Do List.** If you are worried about an event the next day, handwrite out a simple To-Do list and just list the main things that you for sure need to address. This physical process should help soothe your mind (conscious and subconscious) in that these issues will be addressed after your much-needed rest.
- **Lightly tense up your entire body** then slowly release tension starting from your head/face all the way down to your feet. This purposeful process helps relax all your muscles, even ones you might be subconsciously tightening hampering your ability to sleep.
- **Push your tongue up against the top of your mouth** behind your two front teeth. Breathe in deeply through your nose for a count of 4, hold your breath for 7 seconds, then exhale through pursed lips for a count of 7 seconds. Do this for 4 rounds and you should more easily fall asleep.
- ***Visualization***: picture a calm day. The sun is shining but isn't too bright, the sky is blue, and the clouds are puffy white. Concentrate on one small cloud with the blue sky in the background. Vividly see how calm and peaceful it is, utterly still and tranquil. Just as the cloud and skies are calm and peaceful so are you. Relax and simply, sleep.

Many of the sleep tips provided have a combined effect, so try multiple items and see what works best for you.

***AVOID Revenge Bedtime Procrastination:** The term "revenge bedtime procrastination" might sound weird or even made up, but it is a real and common phenomenon. The overall concept is generally considered to be developed/coined by clinical and psychology researchers Floor M. Kroese, Denise T. D. De Ridder , Catharine Evers and Marieke A. Adriaanse of Utrecht University, Utrecht, Netherlands (2014).

The phenomenon has gained a fair amount of attention in that it deals with people purposely choosing not to go to sleep on time even though they do not have work or another specific reason to stay awake (such as a crying baby).

Many people (especially students) know that they should consistently go to sleep at an appropriate time in order to get a healthy amount of sleep (7 to 9 hours), yet they still choose to stay up even though they do not have to. There are many theories as to why people choose to stay up such as lack of mindfulness, low amounts of self-compassion (Sirois et al., 2019), aversions to bedtime routines (Nauts et al., 2016), and subconscious frustration of not having more time in the day due to other factors such as work, school, family, or other obligations (Pundhir, 2021; Starkman, 2021; Türkarslan, 2020).

The term “revenge bedtime procrastination” is also derived from a common feeling in China. Many people in that country experience long workdays (nine in the morning to nine in the evening, six days a week), so they feel stressed and anxious that they have a deprived personal life and stay up (even though they know it is unhealthy) just to have a sense of control = *revenge* against one’s current life situation / condition (Liang, 2020).

Many of us might feel this way and in fact, I have had many students share this same frustration with me. Yet, we have to focus on staying healthy and getting adequate sleep in order to learn and succeed in our educational mission.

Tips to Improve and Help Overcome Revenge Bedtime Procrastination

1. **Reflect:** Be honest with yourself and realize if you are doing this and if so, that you are hurting your health. Google “effect of sleep deprivation” and read for yourself just how you are negatively affecting your health and mental capabilities. See that you need to achieve a healthy balance of work and rest and find better ways to gain control of your life.

2. **Set an Alarm on Your Phone:** Remind yourself that you need to go to bed and follow-through. Be consistent as much as possible.

3. **Turn OFF Auto Play:** whether it is your Netflix, Amazon, YouTube, Disney+, or any other streaming service, turn off the auto play feature to help prevent you from mindlessly staying up and binge-watching episodes/movies all through the night.

4. **Start your Bedtime Routine Early:** Some people procrastinate in going to bed because they don't like having to go brush their teeth, floss, shower, and put on pajamas. Do this earlier so that when it is actually time to go to sleep you will have fewer things to do.

5. **Avoid ANY Type of Screen Time at Least 30 Minutes Before Bedtime:** Sleep researchers have found that exposure from blue light emitted from all screens (cellphones, tablets, laptops, and televisions) before going to sleep decreases sleep quality and enhances one's alertness which can make you not want to go to sleep even though you know you need to get some rest (Ostrin et al., 2017; Tosini et al., 2016).

6. **Read as a Form of Having Control:** Consciously tell yourself that you are in control of your time and choose a good (not too stimulating) book to read. Have this be the last thing you do before you go to sleep. Reading at night will tend to make you sleepy and it is very easy to place a bookmark and pick up where you left off.

7. **Be Accountable to Yourself and a Partner:** Keep a journal of when you are going to sleep and share this info with a friend, parent, spouse, sibling, etc. Accountability tends to help us stay on track and do better.

8. **Share What YOU Have Learned:** Many other people suffer from revenge bedtime procrastination but aren't aware that it is a real psychological phenomenon. You might even be staying up with them. Share what you have learned by reading this book and go through these tips to overcome this negative issue together.

9. **If Needed, Seek Professional Help:** Counseling Services (offered on many university campuses) and your family physician can also assist you in overcoming this issue.

The importance of sleep as well as exercise and nutrition cannot be overstated!

As mentioned throughout this section, it directly affects your ability to function in general and to learn specifically. Master this superpower to obtain super strength in health, fitness, and education.

Bonus Secret Superpower: BE LIKABLE –

Ability to Predict the Future

Description: The ability to be *likable* might seem like a common and simple thing, but it is actually something that most students completely overlook. To be *likable* is to authentically be the type of person that other people enjoy being around and the type of person that they would be happy to help.

Importance: This secret little superpower can have huge results and help you predict a very beneficial outcome regarding your learning and GPA. Be sure to read through all the different aspects associated with this to not only fully understand how simply being *likable* can be a powerful benefit, but to also learn **how** to be *likable* in the right ways for the greatest effect.

Explanation: In addition to you as the actual learner, your instructor has the greatest influence on your learning and ultimately your grade (other students can also greatly help you in your learning). Because of this, it is vital to ensure that your instructor and fellow students appreciate you and to put it simply, *like* you. Let me be clear upfront that I am not talking about being fake and shallow, I am talking about actually and authentically being the type of student that the instructor and other students genuinely likes and properly appreciate for the right reasons.

As funny as it sounds, many students never realize this, but all your teachers/instructors are human. That means that they have emotions and just like you and me, they like some people (students) more than others. The key thing you need to understand regarding this realization is why? The answer is that some students interact and behave in a way that makes them not very likable. This can and often does affect how the instructor views and ultimately grades that student.

The following different *being likable* components might be incorporated into how you are actually graded in your class (see your class syllabus/rubric) but there are often grey areas, not specified aspects of how you interact in class with your instructor and other students. Each of these aspects increases your likeability and works together in a synergistic manner to enhance its overall effect.

***Active Listening:** One of the simplest ways to become more likable is by using active listening whenever you are interacting with someone. This proper way of listening is easy but takes practice to properly and consistently use it effectively.

1. **Maintain Good Eye Contact** with the person that is talking. This means that you stop all other activities like looking at your cellphone and give your full attention to the person talking. If this is occurring online through a web camera / cell phone, it needs to function a little differently since you are not face-to-face. Instead of just looking at their eyes on the screen, you need to periodically look into the camera in that this translates into looking at their eyes.

This takes practice to properly do. You want to look at their video so that you can fully understand what they are saying, but you also want to look at the camera so that they can better feel that you are paying attention to what they are saying.

2. **Provide Feedback** to the person talking by maintaining proper eye contact, shaking your head up and down to express understanding, and, if appropriate, give verbal feedback like "uh hu, yes, I see, ok, that makes sense, interesting." This helps the person speaking realize that you are paying attention and are understanding what is being expressed.

3. **Let the Person Speak:** Don't interrupt. This usually happens when the person isn't listening to understand, they are simply wanting to reply to express their thoughts on the situation. Instead, be patient and let the person fully explain their idea, comment, or question before responding.

4. **Brief Back:** When the speaker is finished talking, a great way to ensure active listening is to, summarize what the person just said in your own words to ensure that you fully understood what was said.

***Promptness:** Don't be late. You might not realize or even believe it but being late to class is extremely distracting and disrespectful to both the instructor and the other students (even if you are in a large class). As a professor, I can't help but look at a student who comes in late and think that they don't fully respect the class. All the other students were able to show up on time.

Don't get me wrong, things happen, life happens. We might all be late for one reason or another. What I am talking about is to avoid being a student that makes it a habit of being late. This type of student, the habitually late student, is now someone that doesn't care enough to properly plan their schedule in order to get to class on time. This equals not being likable.

If you do happen to be unavoidably late, come in as quietly as possible, don't say "hi" to everyone, just find a seat, sit down, and learn. Afterward, apologies to the instructor and work to not let it happen again.

Not being late and even better, being early for class, shows the instructor that you care about the class and want to learn. This then equates to you coming across as caring, respectful, and of course, *likable*.

***Participating:** A great way to win the favor of the instructor is to simply participate in class. By being part of the discussion, answering questions, and asking questions, you show the instructor that you have done your reading, are really interested in the class, and in learning the material. As already mentioned throughout this book, active participation and engagement will greatly aid you in being able to learn the material, but this will also make you much more *likable* to the instructor.

Be sure to properly participate and let others answer some questions as well. Don't dominate the class discussion. Also, work to help others if they are struggling to answer/participate in class. As an example, if someone answers a question incorrectly you might offer support and state something like "I can totally see why he answered that way. I was thinking in the same way. Why is it that X is wrong in this situation?" – This is a great approach on two levels because it will help the student who answered wrong (they will feel less bad since others were thinking similarly) and the instructor will appreciate that you are participating and asking good questions.

***Be Proactive:** If you know you must miss class for some reason, it is always better to let your instructor know ahead of time. Even if it will be an unexcused absence, tell the instructor that you are very sorry for having to miss the class, but you very much want to know what you will be missing. Ask if it would be possible to come in at another time or what would be the most recommended way to get the info.

Showing this type of dedication, preparation, and planning towards your studies will generally be viewed much more favorably to an instructor than a student who just blows off class and skips coming in altogether.

As a professor, I generally excuse an absence if the student took the time to come to me ahead of time and asked for the information that they would be missing. I am generous to this type of pro-active student unless missing class becomes a pattern, or this student is someone who habitually comes in late, to begin with.

This goes the same if you are sick. You need to contact your instructor as soon as possible and let them know about your circumstances. DO NOT wait until the next class period. Email them and let them know that you are or were sick, apologize for missing class, and ask what you can do to make up the missed instructional session or at least get the information that was covered while you were gone.

***Following Through:** Whenever an instructor has to do more work for you or goes out of his/her way to accommodate you so that you keep up in class, it is always a great idea for you simply send a short and professional thank you email. This goes a long way in making yourself likable and maintaining good relations. Here is an example email:

> Hello Professor,
>
> Thank you for sending me the presentation slides from today's class. I want to again apologize for being sick today, but I am feeling much better now and will be there for the next class. I am looking forward to it.
>
> Sincerely,
>
> Student Name
> Professional Communications Course, Section III

Notice that the email is short, to the point, with one thank you and one apology (don't ever do either more than once in an email). Additionally, notice the signature line has the student's name and the specific class that they are in. As a professor, I teach different types of courses, so this is important to include.

***Learning Community:** Be sure to also realize that it is to your benefit to have students within the classroom *like* you as well. Be kind and caring by helping to establish an effective learning community so that everyone can assist each other by way of good discussion, answering questions, and cooperation on group projects, and aiding in motivating one another.

Use proper etiquette and netiquette when interacting with your classmates. Be sure to be genuine and authentic, promptly reply to other people's posts on the class' online forum, and be friendly to new students or those who might not understand it all. Again, realize that besides all of this being the decent thing to do, it is also to your benefit.

As an example, while getting my bachelor's degree I remember helping a fellow student in an expository writing class. English wasn't his first language, so it was a bit harder for him. I wasn't expecting anything from him, I simply helped him because he was a nice guy. The following semester I ended up being in a computer programming class with him and the tables turned. I was the one that needed help and thankfully, he was more than happy to assist me. Thanks to his guidance I did well and was able to understand the material.

Being friendly and kind as well as willing to help others will make you *likable* and will always be to your benefit in many ways. Additionally, honestly being this way will help predict a more prosperous outcome to your educational journey. Remember, it is how a superhero would act and be.

Conclusion

The superpowers presented within this book emerge from using critical thinking to be self-disciplined and follow a logical plan of attack to succeed in your learning journey. Continue to develop your newfound superpowers by taking time to reflect on these awesome abilities. Decide what can still be improved upon and work on that to become even better.

Remember that as a Super Student you are basically a superhero which means that it isn't all just about you. Work to help others and as you've learned, when you help others learn, you also help yourself gain a deeper understanding.

As they say, *with great power like this, comes great responsibility to do good and help others.* Additionally, as I always try to help people (especially students) realize and remember: *Learning, is for Life!*

Super Student Super Powers

You now have the powers needed to succeed. Use your powers wisely, help others, & accomplish great things!

References

Adams, R. V., & Blair, E. (2019). Impact of time management behaviors on undergraduate engineering students' performance. *SAGE Open, 9*(1), 2158244018824506.

Anders, B. (2019). *The Army learning concept, Army learning model: A guide to understanding and implementation*. Emporia, KS: Sovorel Publishing.

Angel, L. A., Pelzella, D. J., & Elvers, G. C. (2010). Background music and cognitive performance. *Perceptual and Motor Skills 110*(3), 1059-1064.

Broaddus, A., Jaquis, C., Jones, C., Jost, S., Lang, A., Li, A., Li, A., Nelson, P., & Spear, E. (2019). Fitbits, field-tests, and grades: The effects of a healthy and physically active lifestyle on the academic performance of first year college students. *International Journal of Sport and Exercise Psychology*. DOI: 10.1080/1612197X.2019.1623062

Brown, K. B., & Malenfant, K. J. (2017). *Academic library impact on student learning and success: Findings from assessment in action team projects.* Association of College and Research Libraries.

Brown, P., Roediger, H., & McDaniel, M. (2014). *Make it stick: The science of successful learning*. Cambridge, MA: Belknap Press of Harvard University Press.

Castlefrank. (2018). *Elon Musk talks about the school he started Ad Astra* [Video]. YouTube. https://www.youtube.com/watch?v=lrBp5BL20Nw&t=159s

Cavanaugh, J. K., & Jacquemin, S. J. (2015). A large sample comparison of grade based student learning outcomes in online vs. face-to-face courses. *Online Learning, 19*(2), n2.

Champlin, S.E., Pasch, K.E. & Perry, C.L. (2016). Is the consumption of energy drinks associated with academic achievement among college students? *The Journal of Primary Prevention 37*, 345–359. https://doi.org/10.1007/s10935-016-0437-4

Cirillo, F. (2006). *The pomodoro technique (the pomodoro)*. San Francisco, CA: Francesco Cirillo. http://www.baomee.info/pdf/technique/1.pdf

Cole, S. W., Yoo, D. J., & Knutson, B. (2012). Interactivity and reward-related neural activation during a serious videogame. *PLoS One, 7*(3), e33909.

Cordoza, M., Ulrich, R. S., Manulik, B. J., Gardiner, S. K., Fitzpatrick, P. S., Hazen, T. M., Mirka, A, & Perkins, R. S. (2018). Impact of nurses taking daily work breaks in a hospital garden on burnout. *American Journal of Critical Care, 27*(6), 508-512.

Covey, S. (1989). *The Seven habits of highly effective people*. Simon & Schuster.

Cuseo, J., Fecas, V. S., & Thompson, A. (2010). *What all first-year students should know: The most potent research-based principles of college success*. Dubuque, IA: Kendall/Hunt.

de la Mora Velasco, E., & Hirumi, A. (2020). The effects of background music on learning: A systematic review of literature to guide future research and practice. *Educational Technology Research and Development* (68), 2817–2837.

Doherty, R., Madigan, S., Warrington, G., & Ellis, J. (2019). Sleep and nutrition interactions: implications for athletes. *Nutrients, 11*(4), 822.

Doran, G. T. (1981). There's a SMART way to write management's goals and objectives. *Management Review, 70*(11), 35-36.

Driscoll, A., Jicha, K., Hunt, A. N., Tichavsky, L., & Thompson, G. (2012). Can online courses deliver in-class results? A comparison of student performance and satisfaction in an online versus a face-to-face introductory sociology course. *Teaching Sociology, 40*(4), 312-331.

Dweck, C. (2017). *Mindset: Changing the way you think to fulfill your potential.* Britain, London: Robinson Ltd.

Friedman, T. (2014). How to get a job at Google. *New York Times.* https://www.nytimes.com/2014/02/23/opinion/sunday/friedman-how-to-get-a-job-at-google.html?_r=1

Gurung, R. & Schwartz, B. (2009). *Optimizing teaching and learning: Practicing pedagogical research.* West Sussex, United Kingdom: John Wiley & Sons.

Hockley, W. E. (2008). The picture superiority effect in associative recognition. *Memory & Cognition, 36*(7), 1351-1359.

Hoops, L. & Artrip, A. (2016). College student success course takers' perceptions of college student effectiveness. *Learning Assistance Review, 21*(2), 55-67.

iCanStudy. (2021). Bloom's Taxonomy is one of the most effective study techniques: Better than active recall [Video]. YouTube. https://www.youtube.com/watch?v=q7lY-FytO3U

Jost, N., Jossen, S., Rothen, N., & Martarelli, C. (2021). The advantage of distributed practice in a blended learning setting. *Education and Information Technologies 26*, (pp. 3097–3113).

Keller, J. M. (1987). Development and use of the ARCS model of instructional design. *Journal of Instructional Development, 10*(3), 2-10. Retrieved from http://www.jstor.org/stable/pdfplus/30221294.pdf

Knowles, M. Holton, E., & Swanson, R. (2005). *The adult learner: The definitive classic in adult education and human resource development*. Burlington, MA: Elsvier.

Kroese, F. M., De Ridder, D. T., Evers, C., & Adriaanse, M. A. (2014). Bedtime procrastination: introducing a new area of procrastination. *Frontiers in Psychology, 5*, 611.

Liang, L. (2020). *The psychology behind 'revenge bedtime procrastination.'* BBC. https://www.bbc.co.uk/worklife/article/20201123-the-psychology-behind-revenge-bedtime-procrastination

Nauts, S., Kamphorst, B. A., Sutu, A. E., Poortvliet, R., & Anderson, J. H. (2016). Aversive bedtime routines as a precursor to bedtime procrastination. *The European Health Psychologist, 18*(2), 80-85.

Newport, C. (2005). *How to win at college: Simple rules for success from star students*. New York, NY: Broadway Books.

Ostrin, L., Abbott, K., Queener, H. (2017). Attenuation of short wavelengths alters sleep and the ipRGC pupil response. *Ophthalmic and Physiological Optics 2017 Jul;37*(4):440-50. Doi: 10.1111/opo.12385 http://onlinelibrary.wiley.com/doi/10.1111/opo.12385/abstract;jsessionid=08F31EB60646DB311B5087B6FDC0FD0E.f02t01

Paivio, A., Rogers, T. B., & Smythe, P. C. (1968). Why are pictures easier to recall than words?. *Psychonomic Science, 11*(4), 137-138.

Pundhir, T. (2021). Correlates Between Sleep Schedules, Mood and College Performance of Students in Online Education During Lockdown. *The International Journal of Indian Psychology*, Volume 9, Issue 3, July-September.

Pekrun, R., Goetz, T., Frenzel, A. C., Barchfeld, P., & Perry, R. P. (2011). Measuring emotions in students' learning and performance: The Achievement Emotions Questionnaire (AEQ). *Contemporary educational psychology, 36*(1), 36-48.

Puetz, T. W., O'Connor, P. J., & Dishman, R. K. (2006). Effects of chronic exercise on feelings of energy and fatigue: A quantitative synthesis. *Psychological Bulletin, 132*(6), 866–876. https://doi.org/10.1037/0033-2909.132.6.866

Oakley, B., & Schewe, O. (2017). *Learn like a pro: Science-based tools to become better at anything*. New York, NY: St. Martin's Publishing Group.

Oakley, B., Sejnowski, T., & McConville, A. (2018). *Learning how to learn: How to succeed in school without spending all your time studying*. New York, NY: Penguin Random House LLC.

Riggs, C. D., Kang, S., & Rennie, O. (2020). Positive Impact of Multiple-Choice Question Authoring and Regular Quiz Participation on Student Learning. CBE—Life *Sciences Education, 19*(2), ar16.

Stapp, A. Prior, L. (2018). The impact of physically active brain breaks on college students' activity levels and perceptions. *Journal of Physical Activity Research*, Vol.3, 1, 60-67.

Starkman, E. (2021). *What is revenge bedtime procrastination?* WebMD. https://www.webmd.com/sleep-disorders/revenge-bedtime-procrastination

Schellenberg, E. G. (2006). *Exposure to music: The truth about the consequences*. Oxford University Press.

Schellenberg, E. G., & Weiss, M. W. (2013). Music and cognitive abilities. In D. Deutsch (Ed.), *The psychology of music* (pp. 499–550). Elsevier Academic Press.

Schewe, O. (2018). *Super Student*. Oslo, Norway: Jaico Publishing House.

Schroeder, (2021, January 6). Online learning to the rescue: Again. *Inside Higher ED*. https://www.insidehighered.com/digital-learning/blogs/online-trending-now/online-learning-rescue-again

Shih, Y. N., Huang, R. H., & Chiang, H. Y. (2012). Background music: Effects on attention performance. *Work 42*(4), 573-578.

Sirois, F. M., Nauts, S., & Molnar, D. S. (2019). Self-compassion and bedtime procrastination: An emotion regulation perspective. *Mindfulness, 10*(3), 434-445.

Soria, K. M., Fransen, J., & Nackerud, S. (2013). Library use and undergraduate student outcomes: New evidence for students' retention and academic success. *Libraries and the Academy, 13*(2), 147-164.

Tosini, G., Ferguson, I., Tsubota, K. (2016). Effects of blue light on the circadian system and eye physiology. *Molecular Vision 22*, pp. 61-72. https://www.ncbi.nlm.nih.gov/pmc/articles/PMC4734149/

Tokuhama-Espinosa, T. (2011). *Mind, brain, and education science: A comprehensive guide to the new brain-based teaching*. New York, NY: W. W. Norton & Company.

Türkarslan, K. K., Okay, D., Çevrim, M., & Bozo, Ö. (2020). Life is short, stay awake: Death anxiety and bedtime procrastination. *The Journal of general psychology,* 147(1), 43-61.

van der Zanden, P. J., Denessen, E., Cillessen, A. H., & Meijer, P. C. (2019). Patterns of success: first-year student success in multiple domains. *Studies in Higher Education, 44*(11), 2081-2095.

Van Praag, H. (2009). Exercise and the brain: Something to chew on. Trends in neurosciences, 32(5), 283-290.

Vedaa, O., Erevik, E. K., Hysing, M., Hayley, A. C., & Siversen, B. (2019). Insomnia, sleep duration and academic performance: A national survey of Norwegian college and university students. *Sleep medicine: X*, 1, 100005.

Voss, J. L., Gonsalves, B. D., Federmeier, K. D., Tranel, D., & Cohen, N. J. (2011). Hippocampal brain-network coordination during volitional exploratory behavior enhances learning. *Nature Neuroscience, 14*(1), 115-120.

Westcott, W. L. (2012). Resistance training is medicine: effects of strength training on health. *Curr Sports Med Rep*. Jul-Aug;11(4): 209-16.

White, L. J., McGowan, H. W., & McDonald, A. C. (2019). The effect of content delivery style on student performance in anatomy. *Anatomical sciences education, 12*(1), 43-51.

Young, S. N., VanWye, W. R., Schafer, M. A., Robertson, T. A., & Poore, A. V. (2019). Factors affecting PhD student success. *International journal of exercise science, 12*(1), 34.

Yu, R., Li, Q., Fischer, C., Doroudi, S., & Xu, D. (2020). Towards Accurate and Fair Prediction of College Success: Evaluating Different Sources of Student Data. *Proceedings of The 13th International Conference on Educational Data Mining* (EDM 2020).

S.M.A.R.T. Goals Worksheet

S.M.A.R.T. Goals Worksheet	
Initial goal draft:	
S Specific	
M Measurable	
A Actionable	
R Relevant	
T Timely	
Final S.M.A.R.T. goal:	

Educational After Actions Review (AAR) Worksheet

After any major training event, big assignment/project, or test, reflect and answer the following questions so that you can continually improve.

EVENT NAME:

1. What are the things that went right (*list the main things that were helpful – example: started the assignment early enough, got good sleep the night before the test*):

2. What are the things that did not go right (*list the main things that hampered your success – example: didn't periodically quiz/test myself in the days/weeks before the big test, haven't been exercising/eating well so felt sluggish*):

3. How can I do things better in the future (*be honest and specific on actionable steps you can take to help ensure a better outcome next time – improvement is key*):

7 Step Writing Process

7 STEP WRITING PROCESS

1. Choosing a Topic

Contemplate, research, and reflect, then decide on the appropriate essay topic.

2. Brainstorming

Come up with as many good & bad ideas as you can. Review and select best one.

3. Outlining

Structure essay into levels within intro, body *(supporting main idea)*, & conclusion.

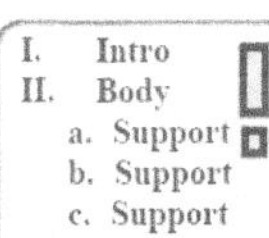

4. Drafting

Complete *(full sentences, almost perfect)* manuscript ready to be reviewed.

5. Soliciting Feedback

Have someone review your draft and offer suggestions (review the rubric)

6. Revising

*Reread entire essay and ensure all is logical

Address/fix all feedback issues and continue to strengthen/clarify the essay.

7. Proofreading

*Check RUBRIC one more time

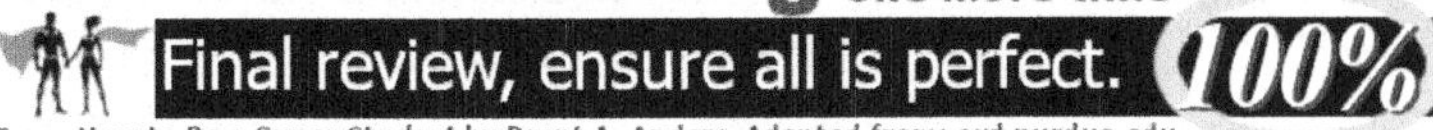

From *How to Be a Super Student* by Brent A. Anders. Adapted from: owl.purdue.edu

Core Adult Learning Principles

CORE ADULT LEARNING PRINCIPLES

Learner's Need to Know

- Need course goals/topics: answer why, what, & how
- Want engagement in collaborative planning process for own learning:provide options when possible

Self-Concept of the Learner

- General desire to be autonomous & self-directing
- Encourage life-long learning skills whenever possible

Prior Experience of the Learner

- Recognize and understand previous experience type & quality to use as a resource and to build upon

Readiness to Learn

- Need to see relevancy/usefulness to real life (now)
- May need changing levels of assistance/scaffolding

Orientation to Learning

- Prefer problem-solving learning orientation
- Prefer experiential (hands-on) learning

Motivation to Learn

- More intrinsic, internal satisfaction
- Importance of personal relevancy now

Dirived from (Knowles, Holton, & Swanson, 2005)
- incorporated with additional explaination (Anders, 2019)

Infographic from the book: **The Army Learning Concept, Army Learning Model: A Guide to Understanding and Implementation**

4-Minute Full Body Yoga Routine

For greater health, 12 to 20 minutes (or more) of yoga is recommended, but if you are in a hurry then this 4-minute full-body yoga routine will still greatly benefit you and help properly orientate your mind to succeeding in what each new day has in store for you. While doing yoga, breathe in through the nose (filling your lower lungs) & out through the mouth calmly.

1. 15 seconds: Walk in Place: While walking, moderately shake your hands out in front of you and lightly kick your legs out. This will help loosen up your joints.

2. 10 seconds: Sky Stretch (Urdhva Hastasana): Reach up to the sky by putting the palms of your hands together and then stretching upwards, going up on your tippy-toes (legs should be about shoulder-width apart). You might hear a slight pop/crack in your back as tension is released.

3. 10 seconds: Chest Stretch (Reverse Butterfly): Put your hands out in front of you, palms together, and then stretch out your hands to the side, stretching out your chest.

4. 10 seconds: Forward Half Bend Pose (Ardha Uttanasana): Put your feet together then bend at the waist and place your palms slightly above your knees. Take in a deep breath, tightening your core each time you breathe in, relax as you breathe out. Do this three times (this will equal the 10 seconds).

5. 10 seconds: Forward Bend Pose (Uttanasana): Now slightly bend your knees and bend over more so that you can touch your toes (or at least try to touch your toes). If you can touch your toes with your fingertips, try to touch them with your knuckles. If you can, then try to touch the floor. If you can do that too, then try to touch the floor with your palms. Hold for 10 seconds.

6. 30 Seconds: Squat Pose (Garland/Malasana): Bend your knees more and spread your legs so that they are about shoulder-width apart. Squat down as far as possible, keeping the bottom of your feet on the floor the entire time. Put the palm of your hands together and push out on your legs with your elbows for an added stretch.

7. 20 Seconds: Reverse Table Pose (Ardha Purvottanasana): Sit on the floor with your legs straight out in front of you, shoulder-width apart. Have your hands straight down to your sides with your palms on the floor. Now push up with your waist and bend your knees so that your body forms a table-like position. Hold for 20 seconds.

8. 15 Seconds: Bound Ankle Pose (Gracious/Bhadrasana): Sit down on your bottom with the bottom of your feet pushed up against each other. Close your eyes and simply think about all the things you are thankful for in your life. As an example, I think about how I am thankful for a nice bed to sleep in, my family, and the opportunity to teach my students at a university. You can also use this time to pray or focus on your future success. End this time by expressing to yourself that you will seek to help others so that we can all succeed.

9. 10 Seconds: Bound Ankle Pose (Gracious/Bhadrasana): Without getting up or changing positions, bend at the waist and try to touch your toes with your forehead. If you can, then touch your forehead with your chin. Hold this stretch for 10 seconds.

10. 30 Seconds: Plank Pose (Phalakasana): Reposition yourself so that you are in a push-up position with your palms on the floor about shoulder-width apart, and your feet together with the palms of your feet on the floor. Your body should be as straight as possible. While tightening your core, hold this plank-like position for the entire 30 seconds. If you feel too much strain in your lower back or arms, put your knees down for 2 seconds then re-assume the position.

11. 20 Seconds: Downward Dog Pose (Adho Mukha Shvanasana): From the push-up position, go into the downward dog position – bend at the waist with your bottom up and your head down but the chin up.

12. 20 Seconds: Upward Dog Pose (Urdhva Mukha Svanasana): Switch to the upward dog position – bend at the waist with your bottom down and your head up.

13. 20 Seconds: Cat/Cow Pose (Bitilasana/Marjaryasana): Move your knees down and arch your back upward (Cat Pose) while breathing in for three seconds. Now arch your back downwards (Cow Pose) while breathing out for three seconds and also tightening your core. Do this sequence for three breaths.

14. 10 Seconds: Child Pose (Balasana): While in the Cat/Cow position, stretch your hands out and away from you, still on the floor but above your head as you lean over more. You'll feel a great stretch in your arms and back. Hold for 10 seconds.

15. 20 Seconds: Squat Pose (Garland/Malasana): Squat down as far as possible, keeping the bottom of your feet on the floor the entire time. Put the palm of your hands together and push out on your legs with your elbows for an added stretch.

16. 10 Seconds: Walk in place like at the beginning of the yoga session.

That's it. You are now done, having stretched out your entire body in less than 5 minutes. Congratulations, you are ready to face a great new day.

4-Minute Yoga (Quicksheet)

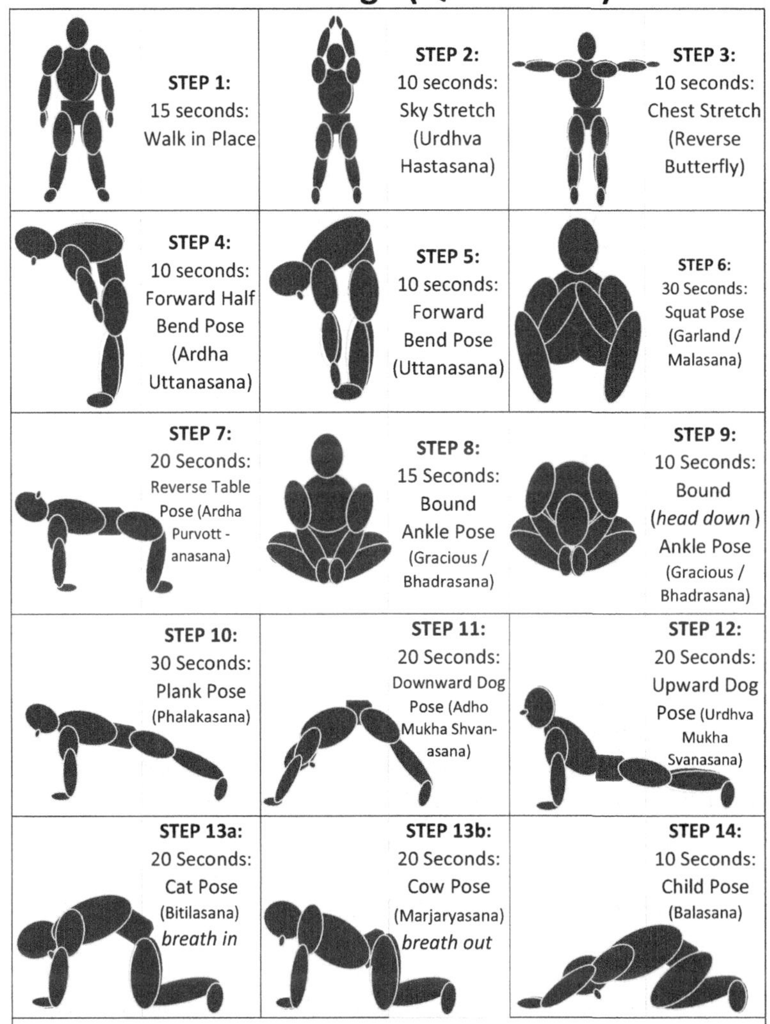

STEP 15: 20 Seconds: Squat Pose (Garland/Malasana) - *already pictured above*
STEP 16: 10 Seconds: Walk in place like at the beginning of the yoga session

About the Author

Brent A. Anders, Ph.D., has worked in higher education for over twenty years, concentrating on digital media, student interaction, and online instruction. Anders has extensively worked as an educational media consultant (video production, live webcasting, student experience / engagement, and instructional technology), a course developer/instructional designer, an educational author, and a professor.

Anders also served in the U.S. Army for over 25 years, first as an airborne infantryman, then as an international certificated military instructor with additional leadership positions. Anders personally trained hundreds of soldiers all over the world, retiring as a Sergeant Major while working with the U.S. Embassy in Armenia as part of the Kansas Army National Guard State Partnership Program.

Anders currently works at a major university in Armenia, instructing students from different majors and helping to establish a center of excellence in teaching and learning. Additionally, Anders authors books and research articles, does periodic international speaking events, and hosts a dedicated educational YouTube channel and blog: www.sovorelpublishing.com.

These different experiences have permitted Anders to observe many different learning scenarios/factors dealing with higher education, allowing him to identify problematic issues and successful solutions. For a full listing of Brent A. Anders' academic publications please visit https://ksu.academia.edu/BrentAnders

Feedback

Thank you very much for reading this special book (it was a labor of love).

If the information was helpful to you in any way, I would greatly appreciate a favorable review on Amazon.

If you would like to contact me directly please use the contact form at Sovorel Publishing:
www.sovorelpublishing.com or
contact@sovorelpublishing.com

Other Available Books and Resources

Seven Characteristics of an Excellent Instructor: Based on Learning Science, available on Amazon (https://www.amazon.com/dp/B0839CXTLQ/).

This highly useful compact e-book presents the top seven characteristics of excellent instructors derived from over 50 scientific journals and resources (from 2000 to 2020).

Each characteristic is fully described, explained, and suggestions on how to develop these characters are provided to help all educational practitioners improve and become excellent instructors.

The Army Learning Concept, Army Learning Model: A Guide to Understanding and Implementation

Available on Amazon (https://www.amazon.com/dp/0998763721/). This book is a powerful implementation guide to fully use and integrate the benefits of the Army Learning Concept (ALC), Army Learning Model (ALM).

Areas covered include improving interaction via enhanced instructional presence, enhanced instructional techniques and technologies such as virtual reality, reaching adult learners, Gen Zs, and everything in between.

How to Enhance Instructional Presence

Available on Amazon (https://www.amazon.com/dp/B06XD2BRC7/). This book deals with how to specifically make students feel more like a real learning member of an instructional community (of inquiry) and not "just a number."

The book describes how strategic implementations of video can be used to enhance social, cognitive, and teaching presence to maximize instructional effectiveness, engagement, instructor approachableness, student achievement, and improve educational experiences.

Take a Walk with Me: A True Story of GRIT and How to Develop it within Your Life

Soon to be available on Amazon (www.amazon.com). "Take a Walk with Me" will deal with the very important topic of grit. It is an interesting type of book because it presents grit through the lens of a true story about completing a 15-mile road march in the Army. It then breaks grit down into easy-to-understand components along with ways to develop grit within your own life.

The importance and need for grit were somewhat addressed in this book "How to Be a Super Student," but "Take a Walk with Me" provides a much deeper understanding and roadmap to success. The power of grit is that it helps us succeed in learning, health/fitness, business, relationships, and all aspects of life. It is a vital component in helping us achieve our goals and true purpose in life.

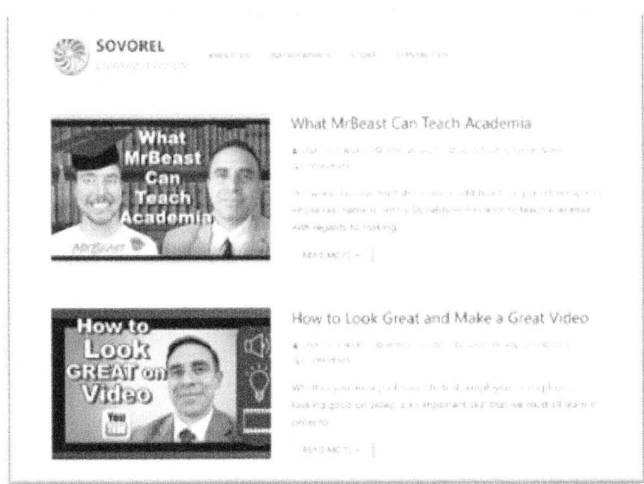

Visit my educational blog **Sovorel**.

This educational blog, along with a dedicated YouTube channel, deals with higher education, focusing on learning, instructional methodologies, instructional technologies, and educational techniques.

The educational blog also provides original, free academic infographics: **www.sovorelpublishing.com**

Thank You

Made in the USA
Middletown, DE
01 May 2022

65057176R00060